Love

&

Space Dust

- David Jones -

David Jones was born in 1989 in Liverpool, which is still his home. He studied English Language and Literature at the University of Liverpool, before specialising in Renaissance and Eighteenth Century Literature. He started writing at an early age, and has previously published two novels and a novella, as well as another poetry anthology. His is also a filmmaker and musician.

For more information on the writer, visit: www.storydj.com, http://twitter.com/djthedavid or on Facebook at https://www.facebook.com/pages/David-Jones/266201170080007.

ISBN-13: 978-1499274813

ISBN-10: 1499274815

"In the end we are nothing more than love and space dust."

Icarus in Love.

I loved you as
Icarus loved
The sun -

Too close,
Too much.

It is both a blessing
And a curse
To feel everything
So very deeply.

They dissect hearts in
Biology, cut them into
Pieces, but I wonder if

They could ever find out
Why you make me
Feel this way.

There seemed to be
Two worlds.
The one before and
After you.

She was not the
Girl of my dreams,
But the girl of every
Waking moment of
Every single day.

An Autumn Haiku.

I hear falling rain,
I hear my thoughts falling too;
All I want is you.

We are nothing but
Space dust
Trying to find
Its way back to
The stars.

After you nothing
Was ever enough.

They could have
Given me the
World and I

Would still have
Been left wanting.

How can it be
That my memories
Are more alive
Than I am?

Is it wrong to be
This young and
This tired?

"All your life is
Ahead of you."

They say, but
Mine feels
Far behind.

I did not want to be
Alone any longer,
So I ran across the
World; lived, loved,

Lost, hoped, feared,
Dreamed, laughed and
Cried until I paused

And wondered, and
Wished to be alone

All over again.

Perhaps we were
Born in the same star.
I can feel the space
Dust in my soul
Hauling us together.

Those eyes of yours
Could swallow stars,
Galaxies and universes.

What hope did I
Ever have?

All the poetry
In all the world
Could not put
Us back
Together again.

I wrapped my
Heart in steel but
You still managed

To break it.

Loving you was
The most
Exquisite form
Of self
Destruction.

Sometimes the greatest
Love is simply
To let go.

The monsters in
My head always knew
That I would
Lose you in

The end.

Of all the people
I used to be,

I miss the one
That you loved,
The most.

And in the end
We are only atoms,
Drifting alone,
Desperate for
Something to
Cling on to.

People confuse past
With present.
They think you are
Still who you used to be,
When that person has
Long since died
Their death.

I look back and realise
That I clung on when
I should have let go,
And let go
When I should have
Clung on for

Dear life.

There is no escape.

The whole world is
Drenched in the
Memories of you.

I have always had
Such huge feelings
For such a
Tiny person.

The sun is out
But I am cold.

My eyes are wide
But my mind is asleep.

The world is alive
But I am dead.

Nature is love
But I am aloof.

Everything screams:

"Live for today"
When I died
Yesterday.

I travelled the world
To find my soul but
It was here with you
All along.

I ache for you with
A pain far deeper
Than I ever thought
I could feel.

For so long

I had seemed
A stream, but you
Found in me a sea.

The universe is
In your bones,
The stars in your
Soul; it's never
Really the

End.

The atoms of me
And the atoms of you,
Will be ink one day,
And paper and pen,
And then, at last,
We will be a poem,
A love song;

Some immortal verse.

The night sky
Is empty.

We dreamed the
Stars to hide
The loneliness
Of the earth.

Do I dare
Tell you
That I love you?

I feel as though
The world may
Fall apart at
Its seams,
The stars come
Tumbling from
The Heavens.

Our love was of
The Autumn;

Heady, golden and
Pure, but limited,
Always doomed

To expire.

I am so afraid.
Time will steal
You away and I

Can already
Hear his hurried
Footsteps.

A Love Story.

"I want to be the most important person in somebodies life for once" she said.

"You are! You are! You are!" he thought to himself an infinity of times, but could not quite say it aloud.

<u>A Mid Winter's Night Dream.</u>

I would try and sleep
It all away, but
I would find you in
My dreams too.

I don't want peace.

I want late nights and
Dark rings, action and
Bright lights, love and
Heartbreak and feeling
And pain. I want you.

I want to breathe in life
And breathe out poetry.

A Chance Encounter With Reality.

I could feel it. Every rushing moment. Reality isn't static, it soars and races, blasts against the skin. That's why you have to forget about it. If you concentrate on reality for too long the force of it rips skin from bone and then blasts bone into sand and sand into the wind, back into space to build stars and planets. That's how it works. The whole charade. Perhaps I was about to become a star. Reality hates us all, there can be no doubt. It wants to make stars and it resents us for harbouring its atoms.

I exist too much:
I feel too much,

Think too much.

Reality is crushing
The life out of me.

Lets get drunk
On the night and
Say all the words
We never dared
Whisper in the
Sober day light.

Like all things in life,
Love and heartbreak
Are far worse at night.

It is in those darkest,
Emptiest hours before
The morning that
The silent sea rises
And threatens to
Drown the entire
World, for at that time

There is no world,
Not really, just
Thoughts, memories
And dreams left
Unfulfilled.

I miss you as
The moon misses
The stars;

Alone amongst
The darkness.

Take me to the morning.
I don't need the sun
Or the dawn; you
Are light enough.

It is not darkness
In my heart, just

Emptiness waiting
For the sun.

Of all the lies I
Have ever lived,

My favourite was
You and I.

Smile.
You are the
Building blocks
Of the universe;

The stars, the
Galaxies, and
You will be
Again, soon

Enough.

Our goodbye kiss had lasted years.

I loved you
Until you became
Words and stories,
Poetry and dreams;

Immortal in every

Book and
Every sunrise.

I always thought that
The darkness in my soul

Was better off on paper
Than trapped inside.

Love Beneath The Moon

There is no greater
Truth, than love
Beneath the moon
And the whispering
Voices of the stars.

Pain may make
Good art, but it
Certainly does not
Make good life,
And I decided,
All at once,
That I wished to
Be alive.

If I could start
Again, I swear
I would re-write
Every word of
My life story.

And sometimes
I wonder, whether
The art was worth
The pain.

Every scar was a self portrait.

To be a writer
Is to be a thief.
I steal people,
Places, feelings -
Entire lives and
Make off with them,
Carrying them away
Into the night. To
Write is to steal,

And I have
Plundered you and
All the world: every
Day and every

Fragment of reality.

Any love is a fantasy.
We do not fall in love
With a person but
The dream of them:
A dream of a dream,
A whispering fantasy.

And when I look
Into the mirror,

All I see are
The people I
Could have been.

People do not die
Of the present, but
Of the past:

Memory is the greatest
Killer in all the world.

My memory is
Stained with bad
And even you
Were not enough
To wipe it
Clean.

Don't wish for
Eternity. You
Would only waste
It dreaming
Of yesterday.

The most bitter of tastes
Is that hint of a life
You could have lived
If only -

Even if my mind
Could bring itself
To forget you, my
Heart never will.

Perhaps love was
Only a drug, after all;
An escape, a flight
From reality
Into dreams.

I tried so hard to
Be everything that
You wanted, that I
Forgot who I was.

How terrible it is
To believe that
Only another
Person can put
The broken
Pieces
Back together
Again.

It was the type
Of love that would
Destroy just as easily
As save.

Truth

In the gulf between

What I say and
What I think,

Lies the truth
Of how I feel.

All the rain in
All the world could
Not wash the
Memories from
The depths of
My heart.

A Madman's Diary

I have lost control of
My money,
My diet,
My head,
My heart -
My soul is off
Howling at the moon
And I don't miss it
Or anything else.

I have shed my skin
So many times.

The graveyards must be full
Of all the people
I used to be.

Happiness

How rare happiness is,
We never know it
Until it has gone.

And then there are
Those memories

Which time may
Never make safe,

Which might always
Remain jagged and
Sore, too painful
Ever to revisit.

I miss everything
And nothing
All at once.

Life only ever
Held me to ransom:
The more I had,

The more I feared
I would lose.

What's in your head
Is far worse
Than what's living
Outside.

You are already
Words and stories.
To write is
Only to breathe.

It is a strange doom,
This life. They feed
Us the things that
Will destroy us;

Love, hope, dreams,
Imagination and hours;

A heady concoction
That we can't live
Without but we
Certainly cannot
Live with.

You are a walking
Metaphor for death
And decay.

Everything you are
And were is already
Crumbling into

The earth.

Don't hold on.
There is nothing
In the world
That isn't turning
Slowly to dust.

And in my dreams
I will always find

My way back
To you.

And in the end
I will seek you
Out amongst
The stars.

The space dust
Of me will
Whisper
"I love you"

Into the infinity
Of the universe.

The Emperor and The Space Man.

On the evening of 1st December 1805, Napoleon's Grande Armée was amassed along the hills of Austerlitz, preparing itself as any army does for the action of the following day. Amongst the bustling ranks, the clanking spurs and the crackle of cooking fires, stood a Spaceman, aware simultaneously of both his mortality and immortality. Across what would be the battlefield, the combined forces of Russia and Austria were plainly visible, but none of the French paid them any special attention. The encampment upon those other hills was an entirely different world, one which scarcely seemed relevant to the French who went about their business as though the opposing army did not even exist. Only the Spaceman, who had already been granted a privileged glance through all of time, would peer across the plains towards the dark mass of the enemy. The French were outnumbered, and conventional logic would suggest that defeat was the more likely of the two results. Napoleon defied conventional logic though, or at the very least he did not care for it, and thus neither did his soldiers. The Spaceman already knew what would occur on the following day. He was well aware of the storming of Pratzen Heights, of the disordered retreat of the Allies, of Napoleon's triumph and the glory of France. Without knowing how he had come by the knowledge, for he had certainly never read it, never been told, never even been born to be educated, the Spaceman saw the might of the Grande Armée, the years of peace, the tantalising prospect of equality and liberty for all within the dream of a universal nation, but he saw beyond it too. He knew of the burning of Moscow, of Leipzig, of Waterloo and finally of St Helena. He saw the dark promise of the future long after Napoleon. He saw equality and liberty evaporate in trenches, in swastikas, and finally in camps behind barbed wire fences.

Vive L'Empereur!

A squadron of cavalry was passing his tent. The shout was echoed from innumerable unidentifiable sources until it ricochetted amongst the tents, collided with the cooking pots and finally soared upwards, a spontaneous burst into the evening air, which must surely have found its way to the other hills. No similar ringing endorsement of the Tsar or Francis came crying back in reply. The Spaceman smiled. He was at peace. Tomorrow he would die, and the game of cosmic dice would commence afresh. Perhaps this time he would be lucky. He had waited long enough.

Daylight was dwindling, and the next time the sun rose it would be serenaded by cannon fire. For now the sky was clear, though, and the moon and stars, marooned in far flung expanses of space, gazed placidly down on the machinations of humanity. The Spaceman would often stare up at those distant suns and planets and feel the lullaby of their motion tugging upon his soul, gently whispering to the dust of his being to return to its home. Tonight, more than ever, he felt the soft, cosmic breath of the universe upon his make-believe skin. It was not impatient to have him back, but enticing, gentle, for it knew it need not hurry, need not haul his being away into the distant galaxies, for it would be there soon enough. The Spaceman had lived in many places through many generations, and he had heard the tug of the Universe called innumerable things. It had gone by so many names: God, Tao, Brahman, Oblivion, but it denied all names because it was beyond words. It simply *was*. Now, as Napoleon's troops moved this way and that beneath the Almighty Was, as birds wheeled and called out to the setting sun over the hills of Austerlitz, the Spaceman felt a closer proximity than ever before to the fathomless depths of the sky, and he knew that he would be returning to them before the next sunset. Pots clanked and the smell of wood smoke was in the air. The next day would arrive, and the next, and then the next - onwards into infinity.

That night, Napoleon met his troops. The Spaceman found himself surrounded by soldiers and with an officer, swaddled in a deep blue cloak, at his side. The officer looked anxiously at his regiment, made some attempt at ordering them into a line, but to no avail. The men were too eager, and they pressed forward in excitable fashion, keen for a view of the Emperor. A trail of smoke rose vertically into the mustering dark of the sky, but the camp was still busy. In the distance a line of troops made its way up a hill, cavalry galloped by and, suspended high on a tree, a man cut branches for firewood, sending a cascade of splintering bark raining down to the earth. Horses grazed quietly in a hollow nearby and, almost lost to the night, a river, lined with trees, wound away towards the horizon. All of a sudden there was a new sound - the uniform tramp of horses' hooves and the low groan of wood: a carriage was approaching. A uniform hush heralded the approach of the Emperor. Ever those on the outskirts of the scene, ostensibly not involved in this meeting, fell silent. Napoleon arrived in a carriage drawn by two white horses, dismounted and approached, followed by a small contingent of Adjutants who, entirely in his shadow, watched the progress of their Emperor from a little distance behind. Napoleon made his way through the regiment, pausing here and there, addressing some of the troops, speaking with the officers, offering words of encouragement to the soldiers. So at ease was the Emperor, that the general air of nerves which his presence inspired, quickly dissipated. The Spaceman watched Napoleon as though he were hardly real, more a concept than a person, one composed almost entirely of a history which even he did not, perhaps never would, fully comprehend. The Spaceman felt privileged to meet this man at such a moment. The vast expanses of eternity did not demean the efforts of Napoleon or the French, for one must live where one lives. Hope is always hope, freedom is forever vital. A mere three men away, Napoleon paused and said something inaudible to one of the soldiers, who smiled and nodded. The

Adjutants whispered amongst themselves and the crowd leaned forward, but the words were lost to the night air. A few moments later, the Emperor faced the Spaceman, clasped his hand and smiled warmly.

The eyes of Spaceman met the eyes of the Emperor, both immortal in their own way. Napoleon looked into him with the familiarity that he greeted all his troops, an amiability which had engendered fierce loyalty in both army and civilians, but for a moment his features altered. For the briefest of seconds, Napoleon's expression transformed into a vague, confused curiosity, the expression of one who has witnessed something unusual but does not quite comprehend its meaning. As though studying a puzzle, the Emperor paused, his eyes narrowed and then, as if a transitory flicker of realisation, of incomprehensibly vast understanding, flared in his mind, Napoleon's eyes widened with surprise. The Spaceman, never recognised as anything other than a man over the course of an infinity of lifetimes, gazed back in wonder and felt his knowledge, his privileged, hopeless view of the universe pressing upon his consciousness. For a fleeting moment he considered telling the Emperor everything, warning him against Moscow, against the winter, Leipzig, Waterloo, securing the promise of the Revolution but, just as quickly as Napoleon had recognised eternity in his foot soldier's eyes, his expression returned to calm amiability and he was gone, proceeding away down his line.

There was a lively hum in the air, even as the sun set. The French were lighting fires, polishing weapons, checking their horses, making their final preparations for battle with such joviality that to any casual onlooker somehow unaware of the situation, they may just as easily have been readying themselves for a ball. The Spaceman had been waiting for this moment, and he retired to his tent. Cut off so completely from the bustle and noise of the camp, his thoughts turned to the future. The infinity of the Universe is such that, after death, after the deaths of planets, suns and galaxies, the space dust that was a person re-forms and, in the timeless eternity of space, chance dictates that they will live another life, and then another, and then another. They will live every possible life, in fact, even the ones they have lived already. In this respect the Spaceman was no different from anybody else in the world, but unlike the rest of humanity, he retained his memories, his feelings. He vividly recalled every life he had lived in that perpetual game of chance, and every feeling he had ever felt. All of history and all of life jostled within the confines of his mind.

It is also true that, in all of time, there will be one love, one particular person, who stays in the heart forever. Everyone has experienced such a love, and most people, the soldiers outside the tent, the Austrians across the fields; everyone, in fact, has loved one person above all others, even if they are currently separated from them by millenniums and inconceivable spans of time. We have all felt this love, even if we are not aware of it. The strange, inexplicable yearning for the unknown experienced late at night, the sense of heartbreak tugging at the soul as we gaze up at the moon or into the cosmos - even those transitory moments of waking from a dream, when we clutch helplessly at a feeling, a memory, an emotion, as it slips helplessly away, all of these sensations recall us to the forgotten past. It is that life, that one life amongst the infinity, the life lived with the love greater than all others, which matters. Over the course of that life, there are moments, too, moments more special, more vital, than the rest of eternity. For everybody else, this knowledge is hidden, the feelings vague and inexplicable, but for the Spaceman, these memories were as clear as the skies above Austerlitz.

He remembered with perfect clarity that one life, that one person but now, now that the end was so very near and the great game would commence afresh, he recalled her not with sorrow, not with longing, but with hope. This time, perhaps, he would find his way back to her. This time, when the universe breathed him back to life, he would open his eyes to that world, that life, and they would meet again in the Autumn, when the mists hovered low over the fields and the sun grew mellow and golden, when the nights grew long and meaningful. A soldier clanked and rattled past the tent, followed by the steady stomp of horses' hooves. The cavalry would not settle. The horses, the soldiers, they were brimming with energy. The Spaceman put his head out of the tent. Some of the officers, their uniforms open at the collar, were reclined around a campfire playing cards. They gestured for him to join them called, but the Spaceman declined. He was losing all connection to this life, and as the hours wore on, the less stable this reality seemed.

He did not share the excitement for the following day, and, while he experienced the thrill that was pulsing through the air, he did so as a spectator, felt its presence but remained unaffected. As such the moment he lay down, his tent faintly illuminated by the glow of the fires outside, the Spaceman's eyes closed and he drifted into a sleep so deep, so pure, that it was almost death. Only his dreams were alive and now, on this final night, they were more vivid than ever. Dreams, not bound by the reality which governs the mind during its waking hours, drift easily through time, through lives, and the Spaceman was carried back through the ages, back to her. They met for the first time, smiled, spoke, lived, and he experienced true happiness, a peace so great that it was so very nearly real.

These dreams were interrupted in the dead of the night, an hour which the Spaceman judged to be midnight. Outside the tent, the soldiers were singing. Vaguely aware of what was occurring, his mind still clouded, fogged as though it were attempting to regain its grip on reality, the Spaceman arose, threw on a tunic and made his way outside. The sky was clear, the stars bright, the moon an icy white.

Vive L'Empereur! Vive L'Empereur! Vive L'Empereur!

The French had lit torches and were cheering for Napoleon and all that the future seemed to promise. The Spaceman watched them, their bodies hidden by the night so that only their torches, a sea of shifting, grounded stars, existed. Such hope, such life. For a few moments the Spaceman wondered what it would be to be like them, to live so firmly in one life, to attach all one's hopes, feelings and dreams to one existence alone, one reality. They were fortunate, perhaps, and as they called the name of their Emperor, the Spaceman experienced a faint pang of regret that he must be thus set apart. Across the battlefield the Allied camp was heavy with silence, thick with the dark.

When the Spaceman awoke the next morning, he took no food and no water. Outside the sun had hardly risen, and the December chill drew breath from the lungs in icy, white puffs. The Spaceman buttoned his blue tunic, pulled on his boots and retrieved his bayonet. It was time to go. The French, busy at their cooking fires, breakfasted royally, drank their fill, retrieved their weapons, mounted their horses and made for their positions. There was not a trace of fear in the air, just that same thrill of the night before, only now it was intensified, so that it veritably throbbed upon the air, crackling against the skin. Even the Spaceman, aware of his death and preoccupied with the hope that the Universe would carry him back to the life he so missed, felt his heartbeat quicken. The dispositions had been dispatched, and the Spaceman's regiment would take positions in the village of Sokolnitz. As he marched, his feet falling unconsciously into the rhythm of the men around him, the Spaceman cast one final look out across the battlefield. A heavy mist had collected in the hollows of Austerlitz and glowed a deep gold as the sun began to rise. There were French troops occupying those hollows, enveloped in the mist, but they were invisible, both to his eyes and those of the Allied commanders.

The blue column continued to snake up the hill. As they climbed, the trees grew dense, began to grow in clumps and thickets so that the battlefield was obscured. Skeletal branches reached out, caressed the blue uniforms, but the French marched on, a drumbeat sounding the rhythm of boots along the dirt track. Every foot fell to the beat, until hearts did, too. The Spaceman experienced the drumbeat as a pulse, reverberating in his ears, his heart, and then upwards into the skies and beyond. In that long column of men, only he was silent. The other soldiers talked with a nervous, excited energy of what lay ahead, of cavalry charges and plans, of Napoleon, Murat, Davout, of high command - even of the Tsar and Ferdinand. On his left, one of the soldiers had launched several brave attempts at conversation, but the Spaceman's mind was wandering, was focussed on everything but the battle, and the soldier, taking him for a new recruit who was filled with fear and concentration and unable to quite abandon himself to chance and fate, gave up.

Sokolnitz was a village of modest proportions. The other regiments were already in place. Blue forms armed with muskets and swords dashed this way and that and artillery batteries were scattered around the buildings. A white stone castle loomed in the distance, stark against the pallor of an early morning sky, its ramparts thronging with blue uniforms and glistening with steel. The Spaceman's regiment hurried to the battery in the town square, took up positions amongst the sandbags and, as the day stirred into life, as the sun rose higher and the birds began to call in the bare trees, they waited.

Like a mighty machine whirring into life, the machinations of battle began. Cogs turned, gears groaned, troops moved and the first shots were fired. Allied troops piled heavily into Napoleon's right flank and, as the streets of Sokolnitz began to ring with gunfire, as plaster was blasted from the walls of the cottages and tiles clattered from the roofs, the Spaceman knew very well that he would not have long to wait. The artillery battery boomed, the soldiers crouched, the gun rolled and then, as if the whole operation were as natural to them as breathing, the men fell to reloading. Another round roared away into the sky, but the sounds of the battle were growing intense, the explosions echoing all around so that it was impossible to discern just when and where their own shell landed. Crouching low, his rifle leaning on one of the sand bags, the Spaceman squinted up the street, awaiting the inevitable sight of Allied troops. A cloud of dust, a mingling of debris and smoke, had already descended, the end of the road was obscured and, as the Spaceman breathed in, he felt the cloud crowd slowly into his lungs. The battery fired again. This time even the sound of the launch was lost against the background cacophony. All the world rung with the sound of gunshots, of explosions, of horses, shots, artillery - so loud that they merged into one indiscernible roar, the tidal thunder of a battle underway.

The Spaceman did not have to wait long for his first sight of the enemy. Troops clad in red came pouring through the dust. The French adjusted accordingly. The line erupted with rifle fire. The Spaceman crouched, squinted down his sights but it was impossible to aim, impossible even to think. Red uniforms bore down on him, voices yelled orders in an unfamiliar language and he fired and reloaded, fired and reloaded. From the rear, an almighty ripple of gunfire and artillery broke, the red wave hesitated, fragmented and then scattered in a disordered retreat. The French gave a cheer, but there were bodies. Around the battery, blue had been spattered with crimson, and more men were rushing in to strengthen the line and operate the gun. The dead remained where they were, faces gazing upwards into the depths of the morning sky, but the Spaceman was alive. He noticed that his hands were shaking, but he hurried to reload his rifle and, as the battery juddered, sent another shell soaring into the air, he waited. It would not be long. The Spaceman had no memories beyond this village, these sand bags and this battery. The end must be near.

The Allies assaulted their position a further three times over the course of the morning, but each attack was repelled by the French. The battery continued to fire, more troops replaced the fallen and the chaos of battle, reverberating around the village, clogged the air with such a dense cloud of dust that the cobbled street was almost entirely lost. After the third assault there was a lull. Those red uniforms fell back and no others came rushing to replace them. The French soldiers sank back against the sand bags, reloaded their guns, wiped their brows, some even began to bandage their wounds with shreds of uniform, but the respite was brief. The Allies commenced a new bombardment. The first artillery shell soared over their position and landed full square on the roof of a house. The building buckled in an instant and collapsed as though it had been made of match sticks. A second shell clattered into the street a little ahead of them. The Spaceman felt the heat of the explosion on his face and he felt the breath of death, too, for this was the time.

At the first shell, the French soldiers had returned to their positions, rifles raised, peering into the dust cloud, but no soldiers came charging into the village, only more shells. It is a strange peculiarity of war that enemy shells are somehow distinguishable from friendly, and the Spaceman listened to the explosions, heard the whistling flight and then the dull thud, the impact, the crunching crash of collapsing masonry. Within moments the village was rubble. Houses crumbled, buckling under the barrage, the road was blasted apart and fires sprung up on every side of the battery. There was no world, now, smoke clogged the air, the lungs, the eyes, and the Spaceman knew that his time had come. The shouts of the French troops were the only evidence that there was any life around him but, all of a sudden, one sound alone distinguished itself. The whistling progress of an artillery shell shrieked overhead. The Spaceman smiled. He had heard this sound before, and he closed his eyes. The whistling drew nearer, filled his ears until it was nothing more than a high scream, descending, drawing closer, ever closer -

The noise of the battle ceased and all those thoughts, those feelings and dreams, previously forgotten against the cacophony of war, came rushing back. His consciousness dwindling, The Spaceman experienced a final wave of peace, for now the game would begin again. He closed his eyes and imagined the Autumn. Perhaps this would be the time. Cosmic chance could deliver him back to her, to those days and, as he died, The Spaceman smiled, he heard the whisper of the universe, felt the stars tug upon his soul. He knew that all the love he felt was space dust. All his feelings were space dust. His very being was space dust, and it would be again.

Somewhere across the fields of Austerlitz the mist was lifting. Allied high command was watching wide eyed as battalion upon battalion of French emerged before their eyes. The Allied left was collapsing. Napoleon was watching. The world was changing and time was rushing.

That night the moon rose over Austerlitz, and the stars twinkled.

THE END.

Made in the USA
Lexington, KY
02 November 2016